Once Upon A Dream

Scotland & Northern Ireland

Edited By Donna Samworth

First published in Great Britain in 2017 by:

YoungWriters Est. 1991

Coltsfoot Drive
Peterborough
PE2 9BF
Telephone: 01733 890066
Website: www.youngwriters.co.uk

Book Design by Spencer Hart

SB ISBN 978-1-78624-733-9
Printed and bound in the UK by BookPrintingUK
Website: www.bookprintinguk.com
YB0298E

FOREWORD

Welcome Readers!

Dreams play a big role in our lives, whether from the worlds that keep us entertained at night to the dreams and ambitions we aspire to in the future, so it was only fitting we used this as our topic for our latest nationwide primary school competition.

I am proud to present 'Once Upon A Dream – Scotland & Northern Ireland', a collection of poetic treasures that will make your imaginations run wild. Among these pages you will find a variety of poetic styles, from dreamworld acrostics to space exploring couplets to fear-provoking free verse. Some poems may leave you jumping for joy, some may tickle your sides, while others may pull at your heart strings as each author becomes their own dream catcher.

The selection process, while difficult, proved to be a very rewarding task and I hope you enjoy the range of work that has made it to the final stages. With so many wonderful poems featured in this anthology picking a winner was another very difficult task so well done to Ruaridh Woodland-Broome who has been chosen as the best poet in this collection. I'd also like to congratulate all the young writers featured in this anthology.

Finally, I hope you find the poems that lie within these pages just as entertaining as I did and I hope it is kept as a keepsake for many years to come.

Donna Samworth

CONTENTS

Tír-Na-Nóg Primary School, Ballyclare

Tom Gallagher (10)	133
Keeley McCrea (9)	134
Clara Lecky (10)	138
Rosie Graham (10)	140
Freya Maylin (10)	142
Leah McConnell (10)	144
Grace Nolan (9)	146
Miguel McRoberts (10)	148
Catalina Sempey (9)	149

Wallace Primary School, Elderslie

Ewan Watson (8)	150
Holly Archibald (8)	151
James Miller (8)	152
Luke Owen Ferry (8)	153
James Patrick Madden (8)	154
Callum Johnston (7)	155
Ross Dunn (8)	156
Poppy Bowers (8)	157
Charlie Kerr (8)	158
Emma McKeeve (8)	159
Millie Speirs (7)	160
Gemma Livingstone (8)	161
Innes Baker (8)	162
Charlie Turnbull (8)	163
Euan Rodgers (8)	164
Callum James Herbison (8)	165
Craig McKeeve (8)	166

THE POEMS

Well done! Your poem has been chosen as the best in this book.

The Stag And I

I am walking slowly,
I hear each beat of my heart.
The trees gently sway in unison
But I hear nothing else.

I creep through the trees,
Twigs snap under my feet.
The birds do not chirp nor do they speak.
The breeze slowly brushes my face
As the pine needles fall to the ground.

Then I turn around
Only to see beauty
Standing in front of me.
A majestic stag, breathing,
I stand motionless, watching, looking
As he stands watching me.

I think to myself,
Is this where I want to be?

In a world so quiet but beautiful,
Alone, so alone, the stag and I.

Ruaridh Woodland-Broome (10)
Merchiston Castle School, Edinburgh

Don't Bully... Please

Once there was an awesome kid,
Kind and loving with lots to give.
One night he closed his eyes
And wished for something; he could have died.
One morning he opened his eyes,
Looked in the mirror and cried.
Why can't I see myself through this mirror?
I can't see me, except everything near.
The next day I went to school,
Everything was calm, nothing was cruel.
I said to myself, 'Can anyone see me
Or am I just a fool?'
I went to my friend and said,
'Can you see me or am I alone?'
Next minute she walked away,
I was sad for the rest of the day.
He woke up realising it was a nightmare
But today was the school fair.
I know it wasn't fair.
Am I the punchbag for the school
Or am I going to be looking like a fool?
I hope not,
That nightmare taught me a lot.

Bethany-Rose Adams (11)
Brownlee Primary School, Lisburn

Untitled

I went to sleep last night
And thought of all the horrid, cruel, disgusting
Things that happen on the Earth.
I went into a deep slumber
And found myself looking into a parallel universe,
Where the grass was blue sapphire
And the sky was green like an emerald.
The sun was as white as the clouds
And the moon was a sparkling flame
Which actually gave me warmth.
The telephone boxes were blue
And so were Dorothy's shoes.
The horrible, terrible, atrocious things were fixed,
But what about the nice things?
At first I thought, *this could be,*
Then I thought, *help me!*
There were so much more nicer things back at home,
Although there was no harm trying to make things
better at home or anywhere.

Evie Charlotte Marks (11)
Brownlee Primary School, Lisburn

A Doomy Night

Doomy, gloomy, dark night
Long, scary, stormy night
Nightmares lure and the rain starts dancing
Flowers scatter and the birds glide into their nests
As noisy as a racing car
The doomy, gloomy, dark night appears
Bing, bang, plish, plosh go the children's toys
Thunder crashes and lightning zaps
Watching from their window, the children shiver and smile
The doomy, gloomy, dark night carries on
The dogs bark at the owls
The cats chase the mice
The waves roar at the seaside
And trees' leaves rustle with the wind
As birds fly out into the open
And children go out to play
The doomy, gloomy, dark night vanishes away.

Elliot Hunter (10)

Brownlee Primary School, Lisburn

My World

I woke up to see
A whole new world in front of me.
And in this world the sun shone bright,
It's always day and never night.

I took a step on the emerald grass
And walked to a candy castle with windows of sugar glass
With walls of sweet chocolate.
I grabbed some and put it in my pocket.

I saw something flutter behind me,
The glow of a magical fairy.
She brought me to an enchanted wood
Where under an ancient tree I stood.

I saw something sparkly and shiny,
So I lifted it up so I could see
And in a flash quite instantly
I was back at home safely.

Lily Alderdice (10)
Brownlee Primary School, Lisburn

What Clare Says!

Hello there, my name is Clare,
I'm so cool, I've got my own pool.
This place is as magical as Harry Potter.
I've got a cool house but everyone has a mouse.
It is in LA which is in the USA.
I live beside the beach and my home is made of candy,
The chimney is made of candy sticks with little trinkets.
The doors are made of Chewits
And the rest is chocolate.
But then there is a bat,
It falls on the floor right beside the front door.
Drip, drip, the tap says and then the monster...
It skims the bat and that is that for the bat.

Callum Briggs (10)
Brownlee Primary School, Lisburn

Golden Peace

I closed my eyes to feel the gentle wind,
Oh all the colours of the wind like the distant rainbow,
Softly blowing my hair forward,
It told me, 'Move, move, take another step.'
I went, I took my steps,
When I did so I got a feeling like I could achieve
Or do anything I'd like to
And see the most beautiful sight.

The sunset it was divine,
I looked to the horizon,
I dreamt of travelling beyond,
I looked at the simple waves
Crashing onto the beach,
The sand like gold,
As I felt the magic of the world.

Lucy McAllister (10)
Brownlee Primary School, Lisburn

Dream Castle

I was walking one day beside my dream castle
When I stumbled upon a door.
I was greeted by a handsome prince.
I asked him his name and he replied, 'Prince Elliot.'
'Well, my name's Olivia.'
We were just talking when...
'Oh my Elliot!' yelled an old queen called Naomi.
'What? I've got a princess called Olivia,' said Elliot.
Before I could say anything she'd kidnapped me.
Elliot tried to save me
But the Minions kidnapped him
So I escaped and saved him
And then Naomi fell off a cliff.

Olivia-Grace Magee (10)
Brownlee Primary School, Lisburn

My Dream Land

I live in a fish tank mansion,
It's a nice place but it's quiet.
It's like a promised land.
It's as magical as a dream.
I wish to live here forever.
The animals are as creepy as a spider
But I love it here.

It's as sweet as chocolate.
I have a normal life here except there is a lot more food.
Pop! I open the fish food,
It's feeding time for all.

It smells like rotten food.
I wish I was not alone
But that's the way I live.

Aoife Geary (10)
Brownlee Primary School, Lisburn

Dreamland

My castle is as old as can be,
Seven storeys up and seven storeys down.
In my Dreamworld everything is possible,
Birds riding lions, five fire-breathing dragons,
Nothing is impossible.

If you want a beanstalk that fires out Fanta
Buy some magic beans from me,
There you have it,
How you're as happy as can be,
But whatever you do, don't push the button
In the Cave of Old
That's very bold
And that's the end of that,
Now, I'll dream up another one.

Finn Sinclair (10)
Brownlee Primary School, Lisburn

Runaway Horse

Leaves are falling,
The wind is like a lion roaring...
Oh, such a miserable existence!
I can't be so low,
So, where should I go?
Oh, beautiful China!
The desert is a rising dough... waving and waiting.
My heart is racing.
Oh, the Great Wall of China!
Clip-clop... faster and faster.
I wonder about my master...
No! Freedom awaiting.
So much colour, so much beauty,
Dancing dragons, no more duty.
Free at last.

Raluca Dubei (10)
Brownlee Primary School, Lisburn

Salto Olympic Team

Once upon a dream I found myself in Salto
Olympic team,
I was so happy I saw...

S urround yourself with the dreamers, the believers and thinkers
I 'm not the next Usain Bolt or Michael Phelps, I'm the first Simone Biles
M essage is to never quit
O lympic gold medalist
N ever give up
E nrich everyone who is involved in your life

Simone Biles - World champion gymnast.

Dempsie Elwood (10)
Brownlee Primary School, Lisburn

Mars! Mars!

I'm scared, I'm on a planet
As bright as the sun.
Impossible! I see the sun far away!

It's orange and bright,
'Mars! It's Mars!'
My ship started to make weird noises,
Bang, boom!

Then a black hole has sucked us away!
And now what?
I'm staying here forever!
It's as dark as a wolf's fur!

I'm staying on Mars,
In a black hole!

Kamil Frydrych (11)
Brownlee Primary School, Lisburn

A Wonderful Destination

A place where you can see every planet,
That's never ever been seen,
A place that you can fly in,
With mythical creatures dancing around you,
Just like leprechauns,
You fly into one planet
And there is always something new to see
Where you always seem to feel wonderful
And as happy as can be,
Giants sing and cast dreams,
All night long,
Ooh, there's another dream.

Victoria Gilmour (10)
Brownlee Primary School, Lisburn

The Great Wild

I can see the savannah so yellow as the sun,
So beautiful as butterflies,
So great as can be.
The trees look so glum
And the lions so great
And so fierce lying on the sandy stream,
Where the little piggies line,
So run little piggies as pink as can be,
The lions will get you so run you must do,
If you don't you will be pig fried stew.

Theo Jordy Tonks (11)
Brownlee Primary School, Lisburn

Once Upon A Dream

Carefully I walk down the road,
I see a car.
I am with Emma Carson.
We are at Starbucks.
We spill coffee on ourselves.
We feel sore and ready to cry.

Jaime Mcnally (10)
Currie Primary School, Belfast

Once Upon A Dream

Clearly I see a fire,
I am with the royal family,
I am at Belfast Zoo,
The Queen screams, 'Fire, fire!'
It suddenly goes out.

Bethany Alexandra Lendrum (11)
Currie Primary School, Belfast

Once Upon A Dream

Carefully I sneak,
I'm with Justin and Emma.
I'm in the school.
Freddy Krueger comes to us.
I feel scared and dead - argh!

Corey Michael Jameson (11)
Currie Primary School, Belfast

Once Upon A Dream - A Tanka

Silently I stroll,
Walking round the scary park.
My heart is racing,
I get to the large, high gates,
I am alone and I'm lost.

Emma-Rose McKibbin (11)
Currie Primary School, Belfast

Once Upon A Dream

Speedily I dive,
Crossing the net I stretch out,
The shot hits with force,
Their mouths open wide,
Courage saves the day again.

Kiane Dickson (11)
Currie Primary School, Belfast

Once Upon A Dream - A Tanka

Silently I spy,
Sitting with both of my friends,
See the happiness,
When we see a paradise,
Hopefully we'll get there soon.

Emma Carson (10)
Currie Primary School, Belfast

Once Upon A Dream - A Tanka

Happily I walk
Up to my massive mansion.
I see all my friends,
They all wave and then I leave,
I feel joyful and happy.

Brianna Carson (11)
Currie Primary School, Belfast

Once Upon A Dream

Carefully I run.
I'm with Emma and Rayanna.
I'm at KFC.
I get hot wings and Fanta.
I feel happy and good.

Erin Margaret Robinson (10)
Currie Primary School, Belfast

Once Upon A Dream

Carefully I spot
They can see I am worried
On my paddle boat
So I look away from them
As I keep paddling.

Chloe Harbison (10)
Currie Primary School, Belfast

Once Upon A Dream - A Tanka

Silently I spy
Something magical happens.
Happily I skip
To the end of the rainbow
And spy a pink unicorn.

Rayanna Johnston (10)
Currie Primary School, Belfast

Once Upon A Dream

Carefully I see
A shark in the sea.
They all see my joy
As I am in a big boat,
As I jump in the blue sky.

Maddison Kirsty Sophie McCormick (11)
Currie Primary School, Belfast

Carefully I See

A dolphin swimming in the sea,
They all see I'm happy,
As I am in a big boat,
As I jump into the sky.

Ryan Cowan (10)
Currie Primary School, Belfast

The Land Of Dreams

Come back, Freya Gracie
I can see some bright lights.
I need you to hold me very tight,
Can you come back and hold me tight?
That is my question to you tonight,
Oh Freya, there you are, you gave me the fright of the night.
Let's go and see why those lights are bright.
Oh my goodness they're flying around,
Look, they're landing on the ground
And now they're dancing all around.
Could they be fairies flying around?
Let's move on now to see what's next.
I wonder, should we text Mum?
No I don't think we should because we are having so much fun.
Oh look, that looks like a chocolate shop
So let's go get a chocolate pop.
Oh and there is a sweet pop in that shop.
I wonder if this is real or is it a dream?
But if it's a dream we will wake up
And we won't be able to come back into this fantastic dream
But at least we will remember the Land of Dreams.

Devonne Fitzpatrick (10)
Eden Primary School, Carrickfergus

Space Dangers

Blast off in a rocket ship,
5, 4, 3, 2, 1... lift-off!
Flying at the speed of sound I will not cough.
Space station just a few days away,
There I know I'll be safe.
I just have to remember there are always dangers
in space.
There it is, a massive ship.
I have a stitch in my hip
And that is okay because I can't wait to get aboard.
Here I am, on the ship,
The airlock opens and so do the doors.
Sirens start beeping, I go to the AI.
I ask the AI what's happening,
But shut were its eyes.
I push to the window to see what is going on
And there it is, an asteroid beyond.
So I rush to the escape pods but there is no response.
I ran to the door but it is too late.
The asteroid hits,
And the ship is blown to bits.
I am like bait.
I survive and I'm still alive.
I get rescued but I could have died.

Hanley Finlay (10)
Eden Primary School, Carrickfergus

One Little Nightmare

There was a land of candy
I hope this is not a joke.
Colourful, fizzy, lovely sweets,
Somebody give me a poke.
There are flying fairies
And dragons and unicorns.
Wait, I see a storm.
This lovely land is turning grey.
I'm in the storm and it blows me away.
Now I hope this is a joke.
I fall into a strange place.
I see spiders and it's very dull.
Clowns are there but they are watching the seagull.
Now they see me and then they smile.
I get up to run but I see that I'm trapped.
Clowns surround me, I think I'm their tea.
All of the spiders bite me,
Even though I'm not a flea.
I wake up and see that I'm in my bed.

Jasmine Haggan (9)
Eden Primary School, Carrickfergus

The Running Clown

I am in a hallway and I see a clown in my room.
I look left and right and I see my brother standing with a broom.
I say to him, 'What do we do?'
But before he gets the words out we hear a bang or two.
It sounds like someone's slammed a door shut,
We turn round and in fact it is a big, fat, laughing clown.

It is running fast towards us but then it falls down.
It makes a thump and a thud,
We try to escape but then the clown gets up.
It starts to run faster and faster,
It says, 'Where are you?'
But before the clown finds us I wake up
And I am in my bed.

Katie Louise Charters (10)
Eden Primary School, Carrickfergus

Famous Singer

I saw you last night,
You with famous Elle and Isla.
We were on X Factor and off went the light.
One minute later the light turned on.
They asked us our names.
We all started singing on and on.
Elle had a lolly which she liked.
They all started bringing chocolate in.
After we started singing we got picked.
Isla started kicking everything, it was so funny.
We became famous singers.
We started walking home and I saw a bunny.
Then I woke up.
I woke up in my bed,
So I went downstairs and got a cup.

Sophie McMeekan (10)
Eden Primary School, Carrickfergus

Me Being A Teacher!

One night I saw a light
I dreamed of being a teacher
Not just anyone, none
Of the teachers had a unicorn
Somebody in my class had a piece of glass
In Eden Primary School I lost my cup
So I looked down and up
There were two news dancers
Who loved to answer
When I won it felt so much fun
When I became a dancer I was done
My unicorn had babies
Then I saw two ladies
Suddenly I got on well
Then everybody called me Bell
Then I woke up
I needed my cup.

Elle Devlin (10)
Eden Primary School, Carrickfergus

Sad, Long Death

N ight is coming, the monsters are coming
I 'll stay up all night
G obbling monsters now come out
H iding in this house, it is me
T here is one safe spot, not three
M aybe blood, maybe it's a dream
A ll night long I was in a dream
R eally close to death now, I'll kill them
E vil kills me in the end
S unny day, my friend sees me dead on the floor, he tells every person there are bones with bows.

Bethany Anne Denyer Howes (9)
Eden Primary School, Carrickfergus

Dino World

I've landed in a world
By a giant swirl
By god is that a spino?
I think I've landed in a world for a dino.

Raptors are running around
My head is spinning round
I see a pteranodon
That's it, I'm done.

Now there was a swirl of light
It gave me such a fright
I felt like an old piece of bread
I found myself back in bed.

Now I go there every night
Because of the prehistoric sight!

Oliver Norton (9)
Eden Primary School, Carrickfergus

The Midnight Hunt

The snow glowed in the midnight moon
And the stars twinkled too.
The pups were going coo.
'I'm going out very soon,' I told them.
I crept out slowly, looking about,
Suddenly there were ears.
A rabbit had just appeared.
I chased it down
And caught it in one snap
But I didn't know I had run into a trap.
I heard the gun being loaded,
I growled and snarled but it was too late,
The next day I was served on a plate.

Emily Young (9)
Eden Primary School, Carrickfergus

Chocolate Paradise

On a calm night
My friends, my sisters and I
Woke up with a fright
In a world full of chocolate.

Chocolate rivers, chocolate fountains,
Tiny trees
High up in the mountains
And little lakes full of chocolate.

All the cute animals,
Small bunnies, huge elephants,
Some caring and some funny.

Evil unicorns, what we dread,
We close our eyes,
Then we're safe in bed.

Nicole Patterson (9)
Eden Primary School, Carrickfergus

Sweet Dream Unicorn

My unicorn - so fluffy, so cuddly,
She jumps and runs, she gives me cuddles.
Every day, every night, so fluffy, so cuddly.
She jumps on rainbows, I didn't see last night.
She gives me quite a fright!
Your pink hair and multicoloured tail
Can be spotted miles away.
I can hear the counting sheep hiding behind the hay,
Through the clouds I see your eyes shine tonight.
I know I will sleep well in the day and night.

Rhyanna Barr (10)
Eden Primary School, Carrickfergus

Fiat Mia Punto

My dream was that I went to see all the Fiat Mia
Puntos being made.
I flew on a plane to get to Rome in Italy.
I went and saw the people putting on the windscreen
and headlights,
Seats, radios, engine, doors, steering wheel too.
I felt really excited and Italy is lovely.
I smelled them putting on the leather seats.
I heard machines and lots more.
'Take this new Fiat Mia Punto.'
'Thank you.'

Oliver McConnell (9)
Eden Primary School, Carrickfergus

Unicorn Poem

Unicorn with swishy tail,
Colourful hair with glittery horn,
All have pink skin, even the males,
Wings that are sparkly when they're born,
Unicorn, Sparkle Parkle, goes around the land,
Warm hair swishing from a hairband,
Glittering, shining, colourful hair
Is swishing in the hay around the chair.
In the night her bright colourful hair shines,
In the darkness the clock chimes.

Leigha Courtney (9)
Eden Primary School, Carrickfergus

Monsters

M y run is pacing
O n and on my heart is racing
N obody is here except a skeleton shaking its head
S uddenly there is a house
T he owner is the size of a mouse
E ntering as reluctant as I am
R esidents are monsters and attack with something that rams
S uddenly I'm home asleep in my bed.

Reuben McCarley (9)
Eden Primary School, Carrickfergus

Dream

I dreamt I did a double backflip off a ledge.
Then I jumped from roof to roof.
I was then in a front flip tumble
As I flipped over a hedge.
Then I backflipped onto a house roof.

After that I dreamt I was running free,
Doing flips off buildings
Going as fast as the breeze
But then a cop said, 'Freeze!'

Owen Iles (9)
Eden Primary School, Carrickfergus

Match Day

M y own ice hockey team
A mazing I was on a unicorn
T eam told to go on the ice first
C rowd was screaming like mad chickens
H appy to win the match

D ead quiet, the team was silent
A nd we were all happy
Y awn, I was awake, what a night!

Jack Robert Marc McMath (10)
Eden Primary School, Carrickfergus

Rangers - Best Team Ever

R angers, the best team ever
A nd wish they will never lose
N ever mind because we are always the Blues
G row and grow stronger each day
E verywhere, anywhere, we will follow on
R unning all over the pitch in space
S triving to get to your place.

Callum MacDougall (9)
Eden Primary School, Carrickfergus

What Happens In Wonder World?

I catch my breath,
I look around,
Suddenly I hear a sound...
Bang, bang, bang...
The gingerbread guards had called...
But when I turn around, I look at them,
They look at me...
When I look right past the guards
I see something standing in front of me.
It is a castle tall and huge, different from the rest.
I walk right through the toffee doors,
Gingerbread walls and whipped cream roofs,
There is a grand red and white candy cane staircase.
I gallop up and hear a noise,
I jump, I scream,
I run into the nearest room, there is a wardrobe tall and brown,
It gives me shivers
And a frown,
The wardrobe starts to open,
Bang! A wolf jumps out.
She jumps, I scream,
I run right through the hall,
It is ever so clean,

It is gleaming.
Run, run, run, there's no time,
if she catches you it will be bad,
She'll glare right through your soul,
Grab your heart and put it in a bowl.

I run through the doors,
Into the woods,
My tummy starts to rumble,
'I think I'm hungry.'

There it is, a lovely home,
Not a circle,
Not a dome,
It is a cottage,
Small but humble,
My stomach gives a great big rumble,
What is that? I smell porridge.

I walk right through the tall wooden doors,
Pass the sitting room,
Walk quickly into the kitchen,
There it is,
Three bowls full of porridge,
In all three sizes,
One large,
One medium,

One small,
I take a taste, I try them all,
But one, only one is the best,
I put them to the test,
I eat the large,
It is fantastic,
I run out the door.

I see a man,
A tall one too,
He is strange,
He wears a hat,
In fact a top hat,
A purple one,
Curly ginger hair.

We go to tea, biscuits too,
He called me mad
But I knew he is truly mad.
Kapow, bang, bang!

I'm in a tornado,
It's pink and blue,
Oh but don't forget purple too,

I hear voices,
It sounds like Mum,
I sit up, I'm in my bed,
But this is truly not the end.

Tia Law (9)
Maxwellton Primary School, Glasgow

Mrs Marno Is As Funny As A Frog

Our house is made out of Smarties and vanilla icing,
It is also a Transformer, into a car, a plane and
a rocket.
We have a chimney that is infinite ice cream.
We also have a monkey and a kangaroo for our pets,
We have every piece of technology there is.
We also have the world's biggest waterpark.

Drip,
Bang,
Slurp.

The fizzy juice dripped out of the bottle.
The colourful fireworks made a loud bang.
My sister slurped her blue and red Slush Puppy.

The snow was creeping down from the cloudy sky.
Apples fell from the trees in the sky
And the clouds were as soft as the fluffiest candyfloss
there is.
You could even use rainbows as hammocks
And you could get stardust from the end of
the rainbow.

George Malcolm (11)
Maxwellton Primary School, Glasgow

My Day As A Witch

I'm holding a wand... It is usually a pencil...
I'm at a Quidditch tournament... It's normally
the theatre.
I'm in Griffindor... I thought I was in Yellow House...
I'm at Hogwarts... I thought I went to
Maxwellton Primary.
I'm Hermione Granger... I used to be Millie Haazen...

I'm playing Quidditch and I'm on a broom,
Next minute I'm in a common room.
I've just been at a yummy feast
And I've just faced a three-headed beast.
Draco Malfoy is being mean to me.
Oh no! Ron's car is in the Whomping Willow Tree.
I've been given the Philosopher's Stone.
Oh, I do just want to go home.
I'm home now, my adventure is over.
I think my wish was granted by a four-leaf clover.

Millie Haazen (9)
Maxwellton Primary School, Glasgow

The Adventure Of A Lifetime

A normal day in East Kilbride.
A wee boy waking up, saw a portal.
Rainbow particles and bows for unicorns.
He walked in.

There, in a click of a finger
He started to walk.
He saw a unicorn and Pegasus
Fighting horn to horn, hoof to hoof.
A white chocolate mouse running into a hole
In a candy palace
With a candy cane bridge going into the castle.
Gummy bear teddies, rainbow lace beds.

Next day the sun was shining like a diamond.
Walking through the forest
I saw a sweetie tree and a sweetie-eating dinosaur.
'What?' said the boy called Troy.
He saw a portal and particles that looked like bows for girls.
'I'm home,' said Troy the boy.
His wee sister was being nice,
It was because I had a sack of candy.

Jack Skene McCorquodale (9)
Maxwellton Primary School, Glasgow

Oh La La!

Paris fills me with happiness.
Me and my best mates
Walking my dog Rosey up the Eiffel Tower.
We are on the way back to my house
To take my ponies for a gallop.
Suddenly everything turns upside down.
All the doors start slamming,
The houses start spinning.
We get to my house,
We fall to the ground like someone's pushed us.
Someone shoves us into a room.
We are trapped.
There is a voice from somewhere
That's talking to us.
They say there is secret passcodes all over the room,
We try to find one.
We finally find one.
We are free.
We find our way out my haunted house.
We try to find out who is doing this.
We do.
It is my dad trying to prank me again,
Everything is back to normal again.

Sarah Louise Reid (9)
Maxwellton Primary School, Glasgow

Beach Boat

I'm at the beach and the sunset is beautiful.
I hear the water gently moving.
I see this boat slowly moving.
Me and my dog are playing in the beautiful sand
And I hear screaming, 'Argh!'
I turn around and I am shocked,
I see the boat sinking slowly.
I tell my dog to stay there and I go to help.
All I hear is a scared girl screaming, 'Argh!'
I hear a boy saying help,
I get to the boat feeling brave.
I ask for their names,
'Amy and Max,' they say, scared.
I tell them to jump down into the water.
They say, 'We can't swim.'
I tell Amy to jump down and I will grab her.
She jumps in and I catch her.
Then a boy comes, he says, 'My name is Shaun,
I will get the boy, go!'

Candice Gaw (11)
Maxwellton Primary School, Glasgow

The Unicorn War

Once upon a dream away in France
It was as dark as coal
The worst thing of all was that we were at war
It was with unicorns
We didn't speak unicorn language
That was the worst thing of all
Bang!
The Pegasus started to attack.
'Unicorns wake up! Wake up!'
Unicorns woke up,
At first they didn't know what was going on.
Bang! Bang! Bang!
The Pegasus were attacking.
Boom! Boom! Boom!
The Pegasus set off a bomb,
'Unicorns shoot with your horns!
Do your country proud,
Well I don't know what country you have but fight,
Don't give up!'
Bang! Another bomb went off.
It seemed like they were winning,
Until...

Díarmid McCreadie (8)
Maxwellton Primary School, Glasgow

The Day I Went Back In Time!

Hannah, Millie, Keira and me were just sitting...
Until *bang!*
A portal appeared!
But where would it take us?
We kept guessing but none of us knew so...
We went into it...
And on the other side there was something incredible...
Dinosaurs!
We all thought they were extinct...
Humongous dinosaurs and tiny dinosaurs,
So cool.
We got to take a ride.
We were so high it was amazing!
We were soon in the jungle,
It was scary!
T-rex!
It started chasing us!
We jumped off and got away, just in time.
'Let's go back home now!'
'Wow, what a day!'
Eventually we're back in my room, so excited
But I didn't want to do it again.

Faith O'Donnell (9)
Maxwellton Primary School, Glasgow

Dear The Man On The Moon

Oh my sweet pet, it's OK, have no fear.
The water is crystal clear
The sky above us still,
Like the sand below.
The crystal water swaying calmly
Shimmering stars out in the distance
But the moon is something else,
Oh what a beautiful thing the moon is,
So rare that it talks to me.
I want to meet the man on the moon,
It would be a dream come true.
But you see the moon, it moves too fast
Every day it goes past, and I just wish to see him!
He sends me gifts down in balloons
Saying, 'I will see you soon.'
I send him gifts too you know,
Saying we will be reunited to the man on the moon.

Sophie Butler (10)
Maxwellton Primary School, Glasgow

Competition Time

C omplete silence
O ver the house
M eanwhile I am going into bed
P ut on the TV then fall asleep
E ventually I can hear horses whinnying
T he horse box rattling and an
I nteresting view in front of me
T he people in the car are all excited
I am nervous, so nervous
O n the back of the car all I can see is Katie's ear
N ever thought I could make it this far

T wo hours
I get out the car and we are there
M eanwhile, I am tacking up, I see jumps
E verywhere, it looks amazing!

Erin McCrone (11)
Maxwellton Primary School, Glasgow

Unicorns Get Saved

Bang... Pow... goes the unicorn's horns
Whoosh... goes Pegasus to try and escape.
How did this happen?
How will it end?
Is this war real?
Or is it pretend?

The head of the airforce
Loads up with fuel
Going into battle
Or is it a duel?

Oh my goodness it's turning night,
But the moon is shining very, very bright.
Look over there,
It's a little light,
Is it going to save the night?

The little light
Got closer and closer,
It saved the unicorn
And now war is over.

Lucy Chadwick (9)
Maxwellton Primary School, Glasgow

The Day I Signed For Manchester Utd

In the changing rooms,
Getting ready for the big match against Man City.
I was putting on my Luis Suárez black Adidas boots
And tying my laces up.

We are warming up,
Play up top,
It is my debut,
Hopefully I'll play good,
I get number 11, my lucky number.

Kick off - 10 minutes in
Pogba crosses it in and I score a volley,
What a goal!
56 minutes in Ibra passes it in,
I score bottom right.

'What a shot!' he says,
Last minute Depay chips it in
And I header it,
Amazing!

Grant Jackson (8)
Maxwellton Primary School, Glasgow

The Marine Adventure

Splash! I am tossed into the sea,
All alone in the dark,
But out of the abyss comes a creature,
What is this adventure I am about to embark on?

The creature is dazzling colours,
With a smile as wide as the sea,
It swims to me and says,
'Why don't you come with me?'

It takes me on a journey,
Throughout the seven seas,
I meet sea horses, turtles and sharks,
They tag along with me.

My journey begins to end
And I start to feel quite sad,
But I will always remember,
The great adventure I had.

Jessica Mullin (11)
Maxwellton Primary School, Glasgow

Shoes World

S hoes are all I can see
H oping to find lots and lots of shoes
O nes with sparkles, bows and pretty patterns
E xciting, I found my favourite singer Perrie
S he said I can buy all the shoes I wish

W ow, I have found my dream pair of shoes
O ut of the blue Perrie says, 'Let's go for lunch.' We went to Nando's, it was amazing
R eady or not we went back to the shops
L ooking for my last pair of shoes
D reams are over, back to life now.

Lynsey Donald (11)
Maxwellton Primary School, Glasgow

Night To Remember!

On the Titanic with Mum, Dad and brother James,
Big black and white splotches going into my room.
It's just filled with happiness.
As night flies over the sea,
Dinner in the golden room.
As days sail through the Atlantic it's the 14th April.
Twelve o'clock I'm getting tired now,
But suddenly I hear screaming
And I hear we've hit an iceberg.
Running for our lives we find lifeboats,
Get on and into the sea.
Mum, me and James only got on,
Dad was one that died on April 15th.

Niamh Millsip (9)
Maxwellton Primary School, Glasgow

The Extraordinary Day

One day I took my mind on a walk,
Really my mind took me on a walk,
Whatever the truth was.

The light glittered in the stream
Or the stream glittered in the light,
There stood an emerald.

The animals were lovely,
I kept walking,
The ducks were quacking,
Toddling along behind me.

I had got to a road,
The traffic was atrocious,
Cars whooshing by,
I finally made it across.

I arrived home after
An extraordinary
But ordinary day.

Kaylin Skivington (10)
Maxwellton Primary School, Glasgow

An Awesome Day

Once upon a dream I was getting corn dogs
Close to the stadium.
We won 2-1.
I scored two goals, more goals that Suárez scored.
I went to college for two weeks.
Miss Beg as funny as penguins doing forward flips.
I had a lot of money.
I had a big house.
I had four bathrooms, three living rooms
And 68-inch flat screens.
It smelt like apple and was a minty blue colour.
We were in the finals.
I scored, I made the keeper bang his leg on the post.
We won the Champions League.

Kenzie Clark (9)
Maxwellton Primary School, Glasgow

The Galloping Horse Trip To The Clouds

Flap... We were heading for the clouds
As the horses flew into a gallop
The clouds turned pink.

We met Stacey as we reached the clouds,
We turned round and a magical kingdom appeared,
I wanted it to turn pink and it did.

A unicorn pink and fluffy
Took a twinkle to my eye
It took a leap
And was in front of my eye.

We ran to the house
The gingerbread house.

In bed I heard a click
And fell deep into the night.

Rebecca McNeill (8)
Maxwellton Primary School, Glasgow

An Animal Invasion!

Australia looks like the Hogwarts Express,
Koalas playing Quidditch matches,
The kangaroos are the audience.
What has happened?
Why are all the animals playing?
I turn round and see a bad group of animals
Chasing all of the people in Australia.
We all hide in a weird house,
It has cobwebs and dark, dusty windows,
Ripped curtains,
It's a spooky house.
Some hero guy gets all the animals,
The animals run away,
They never come back again.

Amy Muir (9)
Maxwellton Primary School, Glasgow

Football Fantasy

I had a dream that I was a professional football player.
I played for Real Madrid
And I was the new Ronaldo.
I got paid so much, I had a mansion.
I owned a hotel called the Best Hotel Ever.
Every person paid £40 and £120 per family.
They had a gym, a TV
And an oven microwave.
They had a private jet to themselves
And a private tennis court and a dartboard.
Their room was as big as the Titanic.
I was the best football player ever.

Stephen Sanders (10)
Maxwellton Primary School, Glasgow

Japanese Dream

I have woken on a wooden bed,
Happy, hungry and wanting to go back to bed.
But there is a neko waiting, her name is Ying.
But I say, 'I need to go my sweet, my friends await me.'
We are still hungry, so we go to a cute café!
Sushi, Pocky and lots of Totoro candy!
After we eat we have a chat,
Me, Sky, Jack, Robbie, Zac, Thomas and Candice.
After one hour we are travelling to Fuji-San!
It is so beautiful and so high.
Sugoi!

Lola Fee (10)
Maxwellton Primary School, Glasgow

My Life

Boom! Poof!
I was in a wonderland.
I was not quite sure about all this
But I stayed calm or was I just saying that
Because it felt like my heart was pounding like a rabbit.
I saw unicorns galloping on the horizon.
I slowly walked towards them,
They all ran away
But one stayed out.
I started to back away
Because I knew unicorns were quite shy
But thought this one was different, or was I?

Summer Mcmillan (9)
Maxwellton Primary School, Glasgow

The Champions League Journey

The fans are crazy in Spain,
Celtic have a penalty.
I'm on it - 3, 2, 1... *goooal!*
1-0 against Real Madrid.
Half-time.
Manager says, 'Amazing.'
Next half 1-1.
No!
Manager says, 'Better defending.'
90 minutes.
Penalty,
Goal!
We have won.
Yes!
We won the Champions League.
When heading home...
Fans roaring, 'Best night ever!'

Aiden McMahon (9)
Maxwellton Primary School, Glasgow

Under The Sea

The dark is creeping up
And my eyes are closing.

I feel warm and happy
Then I start to fall asleep.

I hear my mum and dad
Talking and laughing.

I dream I am under the sea
And a fish approaches me.

The fish can talk
and I can breathe under the water.

The fish is called Tom,
Tom tells me that I am the Queen of the Sea.

Megan Seymour (11)
Maxwellton Primary School, Glasgow

The First Year Of Hogwarts

The night Hagrid gave me a letter
As I went with Professor McGonagle
She shouted my name
For the Sorting Hat
I got Griffindor
I sat next to Harry
For the Quidditch matches.

Eva Beth Kay (8)
Maxwellton Primary School, Glasgow

Dreamland

Dreamland is topsy-turvy
Nothing is what it seems
Carpets flying, candy houses
Magic pictures
My mum is queen
Dreamland is awesome
I will always remember it.

Brooklyne O'Neill (11)
Maxwellton Primary School, Glasgow

The Football Dream

I dream of being a footballer
And to play Real Madrid
To score wonderful goals
And play against the best defenders
I celebrate with the fans
And to be the new Messi.

Aaron McNulty (11)
Maxwellton Primary School, Glasgow

The Days

I drive to my new school
And the massive 50-metre pool.
I get to my first lesson with five minutes to spare,
Immediately I get changed with my chest bare.
I walk up to Lane 3
And start my four-lap warm-up.
After a few minutes we are told to get out,
Then told to get changed,
Darkness.

I wake up in a hover car,
I can feel the soft silk of my wheel,
As I come back to my senses I can hear screaming,
My parents screaming.
I notice the ground getting nearer by every second
And I quickly slam down on the accelerator
And we quickly pull up and out of danger.

At the beginning of rugby we are told
That there is a fire alarm going to go
And we have to go into the hover cars
10 minutes earlier
So in the middle of a match
The alarm starts blowing
So we jump into the cars and start driving,

We get halfway and are about to make a turn
Then darkness.

We get in the ship at NASA
And launch ourselves in the seats.
When the ship launches itself upwards
Everyone screams with joy.
When we break the sound barrier
My vision turns red
And we accelerate even more
Soon we move at the speed of light.

The seat belt sign turns off,
I go to the toilet,
When I get back
We are in the seats for another 20 minutes
Then we reach X-23.

Leonard Scanlan (10)
Merchiston Castle School, Edinburgh

The Best Day Ever

8:30am - Wake up in the bright sun,
Run downstairs like a bolt,
Gobble down my breakfast,
Shoes on and out the door,
This is the best day ever!

9:06am - Arrive at my friend's house,
We go to dark outer space,
The world is like a fancy football from up here,
The moon smiles at me and my friend,
This is the best day ever!

11:42am - Run to the big, beautiful beach,
Dive into the ocean that sparkles like a diamond,
The sun shines down on an island in the harbour,
The white horses in the waves come crashing down on the cliffs,
This is the best day ever!

12:57pm - Had a five foot burger in King of Burgers,
It smells like one thousand rosy-red flowers put together,
The burger looks like a ten-storey tower in the middle of the city,
It is lovely, shame it lasts so short,
This is the best day ever!

5:31pm - Snuggled up on the sofa,
It is like lying on a silk man-made cloud,
I heave up the remote and turn on the TV,
I watch my favourite film with a pot of glorious ice cream,
This is the best day ever!

8:58pm - Jump into my furry glossy bed,
The moon is like a ghostly galleon heaving itself through the clouds,
The snow-white blanket snuggled up next to me,
This is the best day ever!
Shame, it is all a dream.

Kit Nugent (10)
Merchiston Castle School, Edinburgh

The Dark Forest

The sinister forest is quiet and eerie.
Shadows cast all over the forest floor.
The moon is like a ghostly galleon in the sky.
It is all so quiet... too quiet.

Twigs snap under my feet.
Trees sway in the whispering breeze.
The darkness swallows everything.
It's very dark... too dark.

Hidden eyes watch me like devils in the dark.
The wind dies completely and I look for an escape.
A ghostly silence drowns the forest.
It's very still... too still.

The moon glides across the murky sky,
All bad things haunt me in my step,
Something moves behind me, I'm petrified.
It's very spooky... too spooky.

Something moves again, panic clouds my mind
And then out from the shadows.
Its eyes are red and coming straight for me,
It's very scary... too scary.

The monster comes into the moonlight,
It lunges forward to eat me.
Sweating, I let out a huge scream,
I sit bolt upright in bed,
Thankfully it was just a dream.

Isaac Foley (10)
Merchiston Castle School, Edinburgh

The Rainbow Land Of Horrors

I can see the large sign above me
Titled: 'The Rainbow Land of Horrors'.

I can see my trusty cloud,
Nimbus by my side, reading the sign aloud.

I can feel the heat of the sun
On my face as we walk in,
As we do so everything seems to wake up.
I am being watched.

I see the mountain split in half
And a large red-eyed marshmallow,
As big as a blue whale coming out.

I can see the look of confusion and fear on
Nimbus' face.
I imagine my facial expression won't look
much different.

I hear the marshmallow's loud roar
As it lunges on top of us.

I feel shock, I am in bed, my bed at home,
It must have been a dream.

I hear a noise from under my bed,
What could it be?

I went to see what it was,
Or where the sound was coming from.

I see Nimbus,
He must have been making the noise.

I am confused, but he was in my dream,
How did he get here?

Torben Giles Triffitt (11)
Merchiston Castle School, Edinburgh

A Critter's Life

Down below in the ice,
Humanoid wolves playing poker
And scratching all sorts of lice,
Yet planning revenge.

On a hill
A horn sounds
And the enemy
Break their bounds.

Up above an army of spiky critters,
On their backs staring up they lie
Staring at the sky,
Waiting and waiting.

As the wolves smash through the ground,
The critters hide and look around,
Holding something that looks like a pound,
As the wolves thought.

The critters emerge,
They throw their pounds.
That cast a harness
And the wolves sink back to their grounds.

Aonghas Melvin (10)
Merchiston Castle School, Edinburgh

Soccer

I hear the roar of the crowd as if it is a tiger.
I can barely see the ball
As I dribble to the opposing side.
Their jerseys are lit white
As far as any eye can see.

As far as my eye can see,
They're coming to take the ball from me.

The fans cry, the score is tied,
Until I try and score a goal
Just like the great Ronaldo.
The score isn't tied, no fans cried
And we win the Champions League.

Taggart Zanetta (10)
Merchiston Castle School, Edinburgh

The Glooming World

I see the dark forest in my eyes,
Too dark for me to see.
I close my eyes until I see the dark of me!

The spiders crawl up to me,
My skin slithers like a snake,
Bats scream in my ear!

The candle flames dance in the dark,
I hear the breath inside of me,
The stormy sky roars at me!

My last footsteps come to an end,
My voice sounds dark,
This is the last of me
Wake up!

Krish Karthik (10)
Merchiston Castle School, Edinburgh

England Game

The opposition stand strong like a rock,
The hunt begins as I get chased like a gazelle.
Then I charge a boy like a bull,
Then I run faster than a cheetah.
Then I dive like a crocodile,
Then all of a sudden the crowd goes crazy.

I hear nothing now
But the sound of my breath as I take the conversion,
As the ball goes through the posts
My alarm clock goes off.

Lewis Kerr (10)
Merchiston Castle School, Edinburgh

Once Upon A Dream

Once upon a dream I want to be a writer,
I'd write about the police or maybe firefighters.
The police would take on crimes and they would always win,
The firefighters would save people who are tall, fat, small and thin.

Once upon a dream I want to be a chef,
I'd make such sweet treats there would be none left,
I'd cook the most amazing meals the world has ever seen,
I'd be given the honour to cook for the Queen.

Once upon a dream I want to go on rambles,
I'd make my way through bushes and thorny brambles,
I'd camp out at night and watch the stars,
It's the prettiest view in the world by far.

Once upon a dream I want to be a pop star,
I'd have so much money I'd have 50 cars.
All I'd ever do is sing into the microphone
And some day I will become well-known.

Once upon a dream I want to be in plays,
I'd always know what I have to say,
At the end there would be a standing ovation,
It would be such a thrilling sensation.

Once upon a dream I want to have a child,
Their beauty would go on for miles and miles.
They would be little children who are good,
They would always eat their healthy food.

Once upon a dream I want to be a dancer,
I'd twirl and turn my way to being a number
one prancer,
I would practise day and night non-stop,
So I one day would make it to the top.

Though we must awake,
Carry life on as it seems,
We will always remember
Once upon a dream.

Shona Murray (10)
Nether Currie Primary School, Edinburgh

Haunted School

H alf asleep I close my eyes dreaming
A bout a Halloween surprise
U nexpectedly I ended up at school
N ow I feel like a big fool
T hen I start to realise
E ast Currie is overrun with
D reary, smelly, huge flies

S uddenly I start to see
C lowns popping out of bushes like fleas
H owever I hear a yell, it's coming
O ut of a dark smelly well
O ver the hill I see the sea
L ittle do I know I am where I need to be.

Olivia Paden (10)
Nether Currie Primary School, Edinburgh

Once Upon A Dream!

C hocolate doors and some chocolate floors
A mazing candy canes
N ibbles of sweets all over the floor
D elicious marshmallows where people sit
Y ellow and pink Smarties at the front door

H ollow walls where people have been eating
O utrageous candy bars that never have been seen
U pstairs there is candy everywhere all over
S weets decorate the house full of colour
E veryone likes to come to see the gingerbread man.

Lauren Carey (9)
Nether Currie Primary School, Edinburgh

Once Upon My Dream

P ark rider I would be
R ide with Scotty Cranmer
O ff I go to the skatepark
F riends with me
E ssential bikes and equipment
S ent bikes for free
S ponsored by companies
I nternational competitions
O n the first position podium
N ow world no 1
A lways gaining more fans
L ots of kids asking for my signature

B e the best I can be
M onths before
X -games.

Struan Littlejohn (10)
Nether Currie Primary School, Edinburgh

Once Upon A Dream

S ugary cushions that would dissolve in your mouth
W ake up in a house of intriguing joy
E nfolded in these toffee covers
E xtraordinary hot chocolate as purple as strawberry bubblegum
T reats from historical lands

H astily I am eating it all
O rientated by gingerbread furniture
U p it goes higher and stronger
S andy beaches made by glistening rock sweets
E levated birds made of saturating nugget.

Adam McGinnie (10)
Nether Currie Primary School, Edinburgh

My Dream Day

As I fall asleep I see myself at the top
Of a mountain biking course with many other people.
I hear a timer counting down, 5, 4, 3, 2, 1... go!
Getting off to a flying start I overtake everyone else,
The adrenaline is rushing through my body.
As I approach a massive jump I go flying over it.
I rush down to the bottom, finishing in first place,
I shout, 'Hooray.'

Hector Cotton (10)
Nether Currie Primary School, Edinburgh

Happiness

Where am I?
A pitch-black room surrounded me,
Terror filled my heart,
Suddenly
A figure slowly emerged from the darkness.
It was my friend who had passed away,
Happiness overcame the terror inside.
I told him everything I wanted him to know.
With a start I awoke,
A tear ran down my face
But I knew in my heart
You could never tear us apart.

Jacob Creighton (10)
Nether Currie Primary School, Edinburgh

Nightmare

N othing is fun
I can't get out of my nightmare
G iggling voices all I can hear
H urtful in my mind
T aunting, getting louder and louder
M y mind can't think! Help me!
A gonised mind, what can I do?
'R eady to go home?' 'Yes,' I said
E xcited to go home and snuggle in my bed.

Scott Morgan (10)
Nether Currie Primary School, Edinburgh

My Dream Is To Become A Famous YouTuber

Y ouTube is really fun
O n your channel you can upload videos
U pload every day
T ons of YouTubers began little and now they're famous
U nderstanding YouTube is easy
B e strong. If that is what you want to do, then do it
E ager to become a YouTuber? Then make a channel and upload videos every day. This is my dream.

Beth Bremner (10)
Nether Currie Primary School, Edinburgh

Once Upon A Dream

In my dream my cousin
And I were in a random street.
I could hear the supercars roaring like lions
And then I fell asleep.
Oh no, I thought, I won't live my supercar dream.
Then I woke up in the middle of nowhere
And my cousin disappeared.
Wait, where am I?
Then I woke up.
Oh no, it was just a dream.

Adam Matthew Fraser (10)
Nether Currie Primary School, Edinburgh

Singer

S inging in a band would be my dream
I would be a lead singer with my friends beside me
N ight or day, sea or land, I will fulfil my dream
G uitar and drums we play
E very day
R acing to the top, I will get there, I know it.

Aavon Buchanan
Nether Currie Primary School, Edinburgh

Night Sky

Once upon a dream, I dreamed a dream of
Eating ice cream
Lying under a thousand stars
Watching cars
The stars glowed bright
And the moon glowed light.

Soon morning arrived
The moon smiled with kind eyes
And said goodnight.

Zhiying Feng (9)
Nether Currie Primary School, Edinburgh

Alone

A n alley filled with darkness
L oud screams ascend from the floor
O ne step at a time
N oises that no one knows
E veryone is silent.

Jessica Kivlin (9)
Nether Currie Primary School, Edinburgh

My Dream

Going so very fast
Upside down
Underground
Up and down
Then in my bed
In my room
Wide awake.

Ryan Christie (10)
Nether Currie Primary School, Edinburgh

The Multiplying Cup Field

Multiplying cup changes colour
From yellow to red.
Outside in a field
Flooded with burning cups.
Fizzing, crackling noise,
An explosion when they touch!
Smells like burning glass or plastic...
If you touch two cups at the same time
You will experience a peculiar feeling.
I've experienced this feeling before
It drains all the energy, it bites you,
It sucks you in, it burns you, it counts randomly,
It stings you, it changes shape, it twists you,
It shakes you, it sticks to you,
It blows your fingers up
And it pulls you!

Aiden Murray
Royal Blind School, Edinburgh

Weird Call

W orking steadily at my homework
E ábha and Clare are disturbing me with silly text messages
I 'm having fun but then a strange call comes through
R onan my brother asks me who that was, I tell him I don't know
D on't think I knew them!

C arefully I end it, not knowing who this person is
A ll night long I feel so frightened
L ike a very sensible girl I turn my phone off all night long
L ater I wake up with a phone number in my hand...

Maggie McCartney (10)
St Columba's Primary School, Coleraine

A Scary Plane Ride

Up in a plane in a dark sky,
I am up so high.
I look out the window and what do I spy?
A monster with ten eyes, four ears and nine feet high.
He uses his seven long arms to give the plane a shake!
The plane dives down then jolts back up!
The plane goes sideways then the right way up!
Then I hear a bang!
The plane goes down and crashes with a splash into the ocean!
Suddenly I wake up choking with water and smoke.

Sean Faulkner (10)
St Columba's Primary School, Coleraine

The Woods

We were walking along the creepy, crawly woods
On a late eerie autumn night
On the way through the rough, mucky paths we saw a skinny black shadow
Dodging the shadow's steps we were so frightened, Hugh and I felt skinny, bony fingers along our necks, that grabbed us!
Suddenly, I woke up with sweat pouring off me and drenched fists with a broken twig inside one hand...

Eábha Mullan (11)
St Columba's Primary School, Coleraine

My Sport Dream

One evening I had a strange dream.
I saw famous golf and tennis players.

I was with my mum and dad.
I was playing Andy Murray.

My dad was playing Roger Federer.
We were in London, I couldn't believe it.

We were playing at Wimbledon on Centre Court,
My dad was playing on Court One.

With a whoosh and a bang we were off.
When we landed we were on a golf course in London.

I was playing with Henrik Stenson.
I thought I was going to explode with joy.

My dad played with Sergio García.
When we came in we put everything away.

Once we had done that we had lunch together
And we talked and laughed away.

Then I woke up, I'd had a great dream.
I was a bit sad it was not true.

Kyle Robert Steven Caskey (9)
St David's Primary School, Airdrie

Oh Crabs!

One day I woke
Up in space.
It was early
Morning when I woke.

There was knocking
At the door.
It was a giant
Scaly space crab!

I thought it
Was going to eat me!
So I screamed
And it went away crying.

I told my octopus
Octo and Octo screamed, 'Whoop!'
He said the crab wanted
To be friends.

After that the crab came back
And said, 'Friends?'
I laughed,
I don't know.

He told me to call him Eddy.
I think I should be friends with him.
The next day he came back,
We became friends thanks to Octo.

Me and Eddy
Played all day on the swings.
Whoosh went the swings!

Eddy went home
After nine o'clock,
To go to see his mum
And to get some sleep.

Me and Eddy are now best friends.
We like playing armies,
Bang go the guns.

Abigail Tobin (9)
St David's Primary School, Airdrie

The Moon

I had such a dream
At such a scene.
The shooting stars,
The sparkling moon.

I had lovely wings
That loved to sing.
My wings sliced through the air
With lots of care.

My dog Butterball was with me
Loving butter popcorn.
Her little ponytail
That sailed through the air.

Suddenly we landed on the moon
The moon roared hello.
It was shiny,
As shiny as gold.

We danced about
And we pranced about.
It was very fun
And we were right next to the sun.

We added something to it,
It was very sweet.
We screamed with excitement,
We hugged and snuggled.

Soon it was time to go,
Moon said goodbye.
We flew back home,
Too fast so we crashed.

We landed in bed
Very upset.
Soon we woke up
But we couldn't see the moon.

Yana Ivanova (9)
St David's Primary School, Airdrie

Once Upon My Dream

Bang! I wake up with a jump.
I see the sun rising.
I go to walk to the living room when...
Whoosh! A bird flies past me.
I sit up and I'm floating in the air.

I don't know what to do.
I might as well jump off the bed.
Then all of a sudden, *squawk!*
I hear a bird.
I turn around
And I see an eagle coming towards me!

He sits next to me
And shoves me off the bed.
I'm flying in the air! I have wings!
I don't know how to control them, *splash!*

I land in a pool.
Oh well, at least I'm still alive.
The good thing is it's the pool in my garden.
The bad thing is I'm soaked!

Paige Lafferty (9)
St David's Primary School, Airdrie

A Visit To Game Land

One day I was playing on my tablet
When I found a game called Animal Habit.
There were lots of animals like rabbits.

Then it shrank me in,
It looked like a tin,
It seemed like in a bin.

It challenged me a lot of times,
Things like dodgeball, catch in lines,
They were throwing pines.

On the screen it said: 'Next Game',
They were asking me about a name.
It was the last game, what a shame.

I got home and fell on my bed, *bang!*
When I had a sore head, *ouch!*

In the morning I had some bread,
That was a weird night
Which was very bright,
I will remember what is right.

Julia Karolak (9)
St David's Primary School, Airdrie

Magic Dreams

I'll get my dream,
I can't wait.
I hope I don't
Wake up late.

A unicorn with
pink wings.
The unicorn
flies and sings.

Fly up high
Into space.
I just forgot to
Tie my lace.

The snowflakes dancing
In the sky.
I have wings now
I can fly.

I am on a bus taking me
To Mars.
I am in a hotel I can see
Flying cars.

I get a crown I am
The queen.
I'm in a limo
And get free ice cream.

I open my eyes,
I'm awake.
I can't believe all of
That was fake!

Zara Fatama Ali (9)
St David's Primary School, Airdrie

Once Upon A Dream

Dreams are so soft and beautiful,
You're in your own dream place,
it is so good.
I want to stay there,
You meet so many people and land animals.

You can doddle about at any time
and any place,
Pretend you are a wizard,
Swash, pop, bang and *boom*
With your amazing wand
And play until you feel very tired.

You can buy a unicorn if you want to,
Buy a farm too
And stay until you want to meet new animals
If you really want to.

When you go away they want you to stay,
They miss you, and you are the same
And you're grumpy when you go.

Declan McGurk (9)
St David's Primary School, Airdrie

A Space Dog

Me and my family went to space,
It was amazing.
The stars shone as bright as the moon,
We even had a place to stay,
It was called Space House
But we saw something better, a space dog.

It was a black and white collie,
Its coat was as bright and shiny as the stars
And its fur was soft and silky,
It had a big smile.

We took care of it.
It had food and drink and a home
Until it was time to leave,
I was so sad I could cry my head off,
Then my mum and dad said I could take him with me.

Siobhan Taylor (9)
St David's Primary School, Airdrie

Trip To Space

Once there lived a little girl,
Her name was Lilly.
Lilly lived in a magical land
Called Sunny/Winter Wonderland.

One day on her birthday
She had a disco party bus.
Since they lived in Wonderland
They wanted to go to space.

When they arrived in space
They saw a house as tall as an elephant.
The house said hello to them
And told them to come in.

They met some aliens
And they became friends.
All the children said goodbye
And went back home.

Amy Louise Whomes (8)
St David's Primary School, Airdrie

Untitled

I went to the bank,
I saw two robbers,
They looked like a shark
And a whale in a clown outfit.
One said to get out his way
Or he would blow my brains out!

I went to the park
And I bumped into a snake
Called Rattle-Snake Jake.

I was on a climbing frame,
The climbing frame just disappeared
Into thin air.

I was in my room playing
My Xbox with a lion.
He ate me
Because he was hungry.

Shay Reilly (8)
St David's Primary School, Airdrie

My Dream Land

Once upon a dream, in my dream land
I'm dreaming in a happy place
And I hope I'll never leave
But eventually it will be morning
And it will be time to leave.

In my dream land I am a super vet,
When an animal is in pain,
Bang, clap your hands
And I'll come so fast the leaves
Whoosh behind me.

When I get there in a flash
The animals will be up
And running again.

Niamh Crawford (8)
St David's Primary School, Airdrie

Bing, Bang, Bong

I wake from sleep but not in bed,
That's where I'd laid my sleepy head.
I'd meant to rest, but now instead,
I skip along a path, I'm led.
To a magic forest and candy shed!

A trio dancing, they look quite silly,
Singing a song that's very shrilly.
A wizard with golden robes and lily,
An elf and fairy whose dress is frilly.
Whilst swirling mist descends, all chilly.

Some thunder rumbles and lightning arcs.
My friendly wizard, he now turns dark,
With pointed hat and broom he barks.
Bing, bang, bong. As the elf shouts, 'Hark,'
The fairy is switched for a demon shark!

An eerie rhythm, I think a drum,
I really want to suck my thumb.
Why can I see an orange plum?
I wake again, this time less glum.
Safe at last. Held snug by Mum.

Sophia-Rose Robinson-Hamilton (8)
St George's School For Girls, Edinburgh

How Conversations Change

Conversations do not stay the same,
That of course would be lame,
Very lame,
If they did you might be repeating yourself
Over and over again,
Over and over again,
Over and over again!
Don't even think about saying that again!

So if I was talking about rain,
It could change to the seasons,
To how hot it is in Spain,
To how cold it is in Scotland,
To how busy it is in England (London),
To how diverse the world is.
I hope you get the point!

Now the reason I wanted to stretch
This out to the world is because
Of how clever language is,
How clever civilisation is,
How clever my brain, your brain, our brains are.

Conversations move you,
Conversations can make you a giant,
Conversations can make you smaller than a millipede,
Conversations can make you wriggle
And squirm like a worm,
Conversations can make you dance
And prance like a unicorn.

Conversations are friendships,
Conversations are dreams,
Conversations make dreams.

I dream of conversations...
I've had,
I may have.
I dream of conversations,
I hope to dream of more conversations,
I dream of having a conversation with a penguin down a never-ending rainbow,
But that's another conversation...

Kamella Cherise Pollard (7)
St George's School For Girls, Edinburgh

My Olympic Dream

The audience fill up the stadium,
The excited teams ready to compete.
All the flags dazzle in front of me,
In their glorious colours.
The judges take their seats to watch
Every single move you make.

The horses make a majestic entrance,
Girls sparkle in the stunning leotards.
The claps and the cheers ring in my ears,
I am impatient and eager to steal the show.
I look at my horse and she looks at me,
The trust between us will help us through.

We do an opening routine
And then it's all too fast.
I climb on and start somersaults and the splits,
I have no fear as I twist and jump.
I throw myself up in the air,
To make a perfect landing.

Soon it is all over and nothing's left to change,
We take a bow and exit the arena.
Then I wait for the scores

And I hope that I succeed.
Will my Olympic vaulting dream
Ever come true?

Deepti Vijayakumar (8)
St George's School For Girls, Edinburgh

The Land Of Dreams

Dragons soar up in the sky,
Purple monkeys swing and swallows fly.
There is a river of chocolate milk.
I am dressed in the softest silk.
Fairies make lilac flowers bloom.
Down my rainbow slide I zoom!
The sun is a horse whose coat gleams gold,
It is never freezing, not even cold.
There are healing berries for when you are ill,
They are just like a get well pill.
There's no such thing as feeling sad,
No wasps, no nettles or anything bad.
I live in a wood high up in a tree
And no one can say, 'Don't do that!' to me!
I go to sleep in a candyfloss bed,
Snuggling up with Orion, my ted.
I am so happy in my dreamland,
I'm even a member of my own rock band!

Annabel Bruce (7)
St George's School For Girls, Edinburgh

The Candy Dream

We wake up, my sister and I,
The Pegasus soared through the pink sky.
As the unicorns watch by
The blue cotton candy clouds drift high.
Is that a chocolate milk lake I see?
We run and stamp to the lake then, 'Wheeee!'
Then the earth rattles and shakes.
I think it's an earthquake.
We suddenly rise, way high up in the sky.
Oh my, oh my, what a huge tail!
Is that a chocolate chip whale?
We see a house below.
Down we go!
Colleen and I land safe and sound,
All thanks to the marshmallow ground.
Oh what's that ahead?
A house made of gingerbread!
We go in and sleep on the candy beds,
I wake up instead.

Grace Newman (9)
St George's School For Girls, Edinburgh

My Magical Flight

There I was, a Scottish girl
Beside me was my brother
I looked up high into the sky
And noticed something hover.

Against the hill I saw it still.
My heart began to flutter
And with a whoosh I passed a bush
And heard my brother mutter,
'Come back you fool! We're late for school,'
up
up,
up,
But I was rising high up,
And I was in the sky.

I am Queen of the Air, I thought,
Golden and regal.
Not a girl going to school
But a mighty golden eagle!

Anne McDowell (7)
St George's School For Girls, Edinburgh

Fashionista

In my days forward
I hear clickety-click
As the needle punches through fabric.

I complete my own shirt
That comes with a skirt.
They are like sister and brother;
Forever best friends, forever together.

I am a princess of the shop,
I cut but not chop.
I spend my days sewing,
It's all I dream about.

The clothes I create are sparkly
And look very smartly.
The feeling in my heart is amazement,
Like a shooting star in the night sky.

Lila Porphyre (8)
St George's School For Girls, Edinburgh

Lawyer

I want to be a lawyer, not a footballer like Noya
Or a plumber who fixes a leak
Or an astronaut like Peake
Some people might think it's a bore
But I am going to study law
I want to be on the goodies' side
Because the baddies might have stolen and lied
A lawyer's job is an important one
But I will still have lots of fun.

Florence Henry (8)
St George's School For Girls, Edinburgh

Dreaming Of U

U nicorn, oh precious one
N ot reality but myth to me
I n my dreams to you I whisper,
'C ome to me this very night
O ver silvery, soft, magical moonlight.'
R iding high in your mysterious land
N ight-time adventure, 'Oh take my hand.'

Jyoti Amélie Satsangi (7)
St George's School For Girls, Edinburgh

Teddy Bear

Lily is my favourite,
She is a rabbit.
She takes me on a magic trip.
We go to the airport
To fly to Teddy Bear Land.
Lily's sisters live there,
Emily, Isabel and Caitlin.
Their house looks like a teddy bear!

Charlotte Lawrie (6)
St George's School For Girls, Edinburgh

Once Upon A Dream

I was very sleepy so I went to bed
The only thing missing was my ted
I am dozing already, no need to count sheep
For my eyes are closed, I am fast asleep.

As I land in my dream
I hear Craggs Island stream.
As I look to my left I see the plain old sea.
As I look to my right a carno is chasing me.

I swim to the mainland,
I realise I am in a hunting ground.
I am in velociraptor territory,
I think, this should be the end of my story.

I wonder what's happened to that carno.
Him and his scary big bro!
Then my mum wakes me up and...
I think to myself, *what a wonderful cliffhanger?*

Tom Gallagher (10)
Tír-Na-Nóg Primary School, Ballyclare

Once Upon A Dream...

When I was in my new giant house
I heard the doorbell and I was as quiet as a mouse,
My cousin and I tiptoed down the staircase,
At the front door I saw a broad face,
He had lots of grey and white hair,
I blinked twice and hoped he wasn't there,
He looked scary as I watched his curly mane,
All of a sudden I jumped when he rang the doorbell once again,
As I got closer and closer he looked as hairy as a wild boar,
He had huge blue eyes and a pointed nose.

The light shone brightly as I opened the door,
The awfully hairy man looked hairy even more,
He didn't talk and neither did I,
But pointing to the house across the road was his reply,
My cousin and I peered with a really big stare,
When I looked at the house there were dead bodies everywhere,
There were bodies coming out of the window, I almost cried,
There were so many bodies of people who had died,

Then I realised that a body started to get up
very slowly,
Then I could hear someone or something
groaning eerily.

I saw the girl get up, I don't think she was a
human anymore,
She was so creepy I wanted to run out the door,
Other bodies started to get up quite fast;
My heart was racing as time passed,
She was walking like she hurt everywhere,
I wanted to walk closer but I wouldn't dare,
I was so happy it was a dream,
When I wake up I'll let out a huge scream,
I just realised outside there were big, bad zombies!
'I'll fight them off with smelly cheese and bumblebees!'

The other people were zombies as well,
Now the air started to really, really smell,
The green zombie was bashing and smashing at the
great, grand front door,
The other zombies came and did more and more
and more.
I locked the door and ran upstairs and hid under
my bed.
I cuddled into the cosy blanket which was pink and red.
I slowly made my way to turn on the light.

All of a sudden the light turned on and it was
very bright.
My cousin and I were very scared when we looked
through the glass,
We saw lots of zombies on our great green grass.

When I heard the floorboards creak
I let out a huge scream.
The window downstairs was getting bashed
Then I heard it had been smashed.
So I heard the zombies' horrible moan
I started to really, really groan.
I tried to be brave but it was really hard,
It was difficult because there were zombies in my yard!

I heard a zombie come up the staircase
That meant I could see her green, wrinkled, old face.
I now realised that it was eerily handy to have a
big house,
It was handy because I could hide in places as quietly
as a mouse.
As I ran with my cousin up to the fourth floor
I heard banging on the bedroom door,
The zombie managed to get into the room,
I said to myself, 'I am really, really doomed!'
My cousin was trapped with the biggest zombie in
front of her,

I was so scared, everything was a blur,
All of a sudden my cousin's head ripped right off her skull!
This dream was definitely not dull!

She was now a zombie!
This was really, really scary,
I knew it was my turn to die,
Oh why, why, why?
I woke up as I said with a huge scream,
I definitely didn't wake up with a beam!

Keeley McCrea (9)
Tír-Na-Nóg Primary School, Ballyclare

Once Upon A Dream

Once upon a dream I was in a classroom,
Doing all my work.
Be prepared for what will happen next,
It's really quite berserk!

The teacher was teaching us boring maths,
It was so boring I dozed off to sleep.
The teacher was so busy she didn't notice
Luckily she had to answer the phone
When it went *beep! Beep! Beep!*

I was in a big world,
With people the size of giants.
I was still sitting in the classroom when I suddenly twirled,
I was getting teleported to another dimension!

I was in a different place,
With whipped cream on my face.
I found a girl coming towards me,
I was so scared since I was so tiny.

When the girl approached she said
She wanted to be my friend.
I said, 'Yes,' then I told her my name,
This might even be my lead to fame!

We went inside the soda can,
I walked past many desserts, including pear flan.
We went through the tunnel underground,
When the soda popped it made an amazing sound!

I woke up the next morning
To find I was still in the dream.
I tried to wake up in my classroom again,
But I was stuck in this sweet heaven!

I woke my friend (her name is Freya)
And she squirted up in the air.
She was still tucked up in her bed,
When she woke up she had crazy hair!

I started shrinking and I spun again,
I was away from sweets and candy canes!
I was back in the classroom doing maths,
Working out on my sheet of halves.

I thought it was really time for break,
But I woke up in my bed wide awake.
I pinched myself to make sure it wasn't a dream,
I was in normal life, it was all just a dream.

Clara Lecky (10)
Tír-Na-Nóg Primary School, Ballyclare

Once Upon A Dream...

Once upon a dream I found myself in a police car,
I was all dressed in green,
Why am I here? I thought.

I was excited, wondering where I was though...
I was getting very worried,
Just then I realised I was in a dream, I told myself so,
Now I understood everything!

As I opened the boot
A massive bloodhound bounded out,
Quickly, I realised, tied to his collar was a note about stolen loot,
Oh no, I was a policewoman,
I had to go on a mission!

Even though I knew this was a dream,
I was starting to feel very worried and nervous,
Then, I told myself not to worry,
I was on the police team,
So off I set with my dog named Tinker.

According to the note
I had to go to the police station,

When I arrived they told me I was undercover on a boat,
So off I set with my team, a policewoman called Elle.

We lived on the sparkling blue sea,
On a massive, huge and giant white yacht.
As I was reading a book propped on my knee,
I glanced out to the land we were approaching.

After a few long tiring days
We came across a big brown boat,
Then Elle turned as white as a sheet and did say,
'That's the bank robber, the criminal, we've found him, we've found him, yeah!'

After that moment I awoke in my bed
And for the umpteenth time that night I realised that this was a dream,
So I got up and said,
'What an amazing dream!'

Rosie Graham (10)
Tír-Na-Nóg Primary School, Ballyclare

Once Upon A Dream

I looked over Sweetlands,
I saw many sweets, up to thousands.
We live in a soda can under the ground.
When we opened the door it looked so amazing inside.

I was walking on Sweetlands
Then suddenly someone appeared.
I looked around the corner and saw a person.
It was a girl.
She was in a uniform.
I slowly leaned forward and asked her name.
'It is Clara.'
I replied, 'My name is Freya.'

Then I showed Clara the sweet village,
Then I showed Clara my house.
We had to climb up a ladder.
Then I showed her the kitchen,
The tap was running with sparkling soda.

I took Clara to see my room.
The beds were full of soda.
We then skipped to Candyland theme park.

It had a lollipop pool and M&M roller coaster.
We loved the chocolate buttons obstacle course
And jumping with strawberry laces as rope swings.

There was a candyfloss ride with pink, blue and green fluff.
It was so cool, I just loved the stuff!
We got a cone of ice cream in the frozen forest,
Chocolate for me with choc mint for Clara.
After that fun-filled day we jumped into my comfy soda bed and, *bang!*
I was wide awake lying in my own dull, boring bed.
What a dream I had!

Freya Maylin (10)
Tír-Na-Nóg Primary School, Ballyclare

Once Upon A Dream

One night I fell asleep in my bed
I was resting my little head
The next day at seven o'clock
My mum woke me up in a shock
I was wondering what was wrong with her head
'There are new people moving in,' she said
They were across the road,
I was so excited I could explode
We arrived at their house to a scare
I was so scared I wished I wasn't there
I thought for a second, *they will invite us for tea*
Or even worse have us for tea!
We were terrified and shaking
But they actually invited us in with a greeting
We went inside, the little girl looked at me
'Let's go to the table and have some tea.'

Years have passed, I'm still friends with the girl
I go over to her house for a dance, a twirl and even a curl
The next day it was so rainy I didn't know what to say
My family and I decided to watch the news
I heard the news reporter say,
'Oh no, there are some creepy creatures that look like zombies!'

Maybe I could fight them with my smelly cheese
I wanted to look outside, have a little peek
What if they were nice zombies
Maybe they wanted to play hide-and-seek
I woke up in my nice, comfy bed
'Time to get up my sleepyhead,' said Mum.

Leah McConnell (10)
Tír-Na-Nóg Primary School, Ballyclare

Once Upon A Dream

We're driving through the rain
It's pittering and pattering against the window
I start to feel drowsy and warm.

I wake up and I'm still in the car
It's sunny and warm outside
The daffodils are blooming
There's golden corn in the fields once again
Excitement grows in my stomach as I see the sea
As I see the heat gradually melt the powdery snow
On the mountain high above us.

We arrive at a house
With a hedge of flowers
The house is massive
And covered in tiny white stones
I can smell the sea
I hear distant voices
But I am so close to opening the door
I don't want to wake up
My mind is closing
The house is getting further and further away
Everything is getting brighter

I can feel the cold rain skim the surface of my face
As I am hoisted over my father's shoulder
I am carried into a house
Like the one I am in in my dream.

Grace Nolan (9)
Tír-Na-Nóg Primary School, Ballyclare

A Drop Of Genetics And Fusion

I wake up with a light head,
I fear I may be dead,
Soon I see a blinding flash,
Then out of a glowing pipe
A vile-smelling creature comes out to lash
One crazy-haired man,
To be honest, he kind of looks like my gran,
He takes a syringe coloured green
And stabs it into the creature that looks very mean,
Then, another scientist comes over to grab me,
He sure as heck smells like pee,
The crazy-haired guy grabs another one
And stuffs us both into what looks like a blue hot dog bun,
The normal-haired guy then pulls a lever,
I soon wake up to reality,
I hope I don't dream about that again, never...

Miguel McRoberts (10)
Tír-Na-Nóg Primary School, Ballyclare

Once Upon A Dream

Once upon a dream
I was in bed all tucked up,
Having a dream about a cup.
There was hot sauce filled to the brim,
I was doing a challenge with my friend Tim.
We had to see who would drink the most hot sauce,
I did it like a boss.
I won in the end,
I was really lucky,
I did another challenge and it was really mucky.
I was running outside and my friend set me a dare,
I don't care.
I was in my bedroom, playing with my dolls
When my brother brought me balls.
I was at the park and I heard a dog bark.
I was on the slide,
I nearly died.

Catalina Sempey (9)
Tír-Na-Nóg Primary School, Ballyclare

The Adventure!

Tigers, tigers in the night
They will give you one big fright.
If you try to hunt them down
You will end up with a frown
And when you hunt
You will grunt
Because you can't find it,
You keep going bit by bit.
Floating to the atmosphere,
Here we take a quick peer.
Slowly back on land
To play with the sand.
Now I crumble to the ground,
The surface suddenly goes pound!
And something new has been found
Because that is a new sound.

Ewan Watson (8)
Wallace Primary School, Elderslie

In A Gymnastics Competition

Here I am in my bed,
Dreams float all around my head.

There I am, in a gymnastics competition,
Signing up for the audition.
Here I stand, in my leotard,
I know this will not be hard.

After it's done, I hear the crowd go wild,
And the biggest cheer from a little child.
Now it's time to get my medal,
And it's just like a small pebble.

Suddenly waking me up is Mum,
That dream was lots of fun!

Holly Archibald (8)
Wallace Primary School, Elderslie

Crashing On Mars

Once I had a dream
That I was on a space bus
Going to loads of planets.

Loads of aliens
So much fun in space
Mars, Venus, Jupiter, Saturn.

Crash! Bang!
Oh no, the bus crashed
We were stuck.

We were on Mars
Aliens were everywhere
Now they were coming.

We soon had a new bus
We were back on Earth
And the trees were waving.

James Miller (8)
Wallace Primary School, Elderslie

In My Dreams

I went in a portal to another land
N ext I saw lots of Pokémon

M y journey had begun
Y ay, my own Pokémon

D on't go Pikachu
R un Pikachu, I saw Mewtwo
E ek, Master Ball go! I caught Mewtwo!
A trainer; better battle
M y dream was almost over
S o good morning and goodbye.

Luke Owen Ferry (8)
Wallace Primary School, Elderslie

Outer Space

S tars are awesome
P lanets live in the galaxy
A steroids crash down to Earth
C reatures still to be discovered
E arth is the only planet with life

T ravelling with my friends
R ich and scary aliens
A dventure in outer space
V iolent aliens
E xtremely big
L oud as a giant stepping.

James Patrick Madden (8)
Wallace Primary School, Elderslie

Dragon Land

A bsolute danger to come
D ragons fly around you
V ery nice treasure if you get past
E scape as the dragon talks to you
N ever ever going back there
T he sky is slowly turning red
U nicorns dance on rainbows while panicking
R eflecting fire balls hitting the dragon
E veryone is saved from the dragon.

Callum Johnston (7)
Wallace Primary School, Elderslie

Candy Land

C louds are made of candyfloss
A house is like a gingerbread house
N o one is allowed if they're not chocolate
D isgusting candy goes in the candy bin
Y ou can own the candy land

L iquorice is like toxic waste
A nd everyone is colourful
N utella is a river
D ark chocolate is the walls.

Ross Dunn (8)
Wallace Primary School, Elderslie

My Gymnastics Dream

Once upon a time I had a dream
That I could dance along a beam
Like a gymnast fit and strong,
I would cartwheel all day long,
Round-offs, backflips would be no trouble,
I could do them on the double,
Handsprings and dismount on the beam,
Would be easy for me it would seem,
I wish I didn't wake up from my dream.

Poppy Bowers (8)
Wallace Primary School, Elderslie

Dreamland

D reams can be good sometimes
R eading in your mind
E veryone has dreams
A bout unicorns or something happy
M y dreams can be scary
L ate at night you might wake up
A nd you might stay asleep
N ext night you might have a good dream
D readful things can happen.

Charlie Kerr (8)
Wallace Primary School, Elderslie

In The Clouds

There I was cosy in my bed
With my fluffy teddy bear.
Mum said, 'Sweet dreams,'
Then I drifted off to sleep,
I jumped into Candy World
And flew to some candy unicorns
And some sweet, sweet fairies.
The fairies were like tiny gingerbread men,
I jumped out of my comfy bed
And glided off to school.

Emma McKeeve (8)
Wallace Primary School, Elderslie

The Middle Of The Night

I closed my eyes very tight,
It was the middle of the night,
I heard a noise that made me hide,
But then I opened my eyes wide,
I looked around but it was dark,
I thought that I could see a shark!

But no it would really just seem
That it was all just a dream!

Millie Speirs (7)
Wallace Primary School, Elderslie

Riding A Horse In A Race/Riding

R iding a horse is scary
I love it as much as candyfloss
D ecisions to make my horse go fast or slow
I decide to go slow
N ext thing I know I am in first
G alloping past, winning the gold medal and the
trophies.

Gemma Livingstone (8)
Wallace Primary School, Elderslie

Nightmares

D readful things happen at night
R eally it's spooky
E erie sounds echo around
A scary figure of a clown comes out
M ountains growl at me
S uddenly I wake up and realise I am at home safe in bed.

Innes Baker (8)
Wallace Primary School, Elderslie

Dancing

D ancing is fun
A nd dancing is cool
N ervous I am more than you
C ome along to this dance
I 'll never get another chance
N ever at all
G ood luck to you, good luck on the ball.

Charlie Turnbull (8)
Wallace Primary School, Elderslie

Dreams Can...

Dreams can be happy
And dreams can be sad.
Dreams can be fearful
And dreams can be disgusting.
Dreams can be crazy
And dreams can be evil.
Dreams can be like lightning
And dreams can be like clouds.

Euan Rodgers (8)
Wallace Primary School, Elderslie

In My Bed

D rifting into my sleep
R ealising I am in a dream
E xcellent sights I see
A mazing animals
M assive buildings
S uddenly I wake up happy that I am in my bed.

Callum James Herbison (8)
Wallace Primary School, Elderslie

Mice Can...

Mice can eat
And mice can bounce.
Mice can sit
And pounce, pounce, pounce.
Mice have bones
And mice can bite.
Mice can jump
And have a fight.

Craig McKeeve (8)
Wallace Primary School, Elderslie

YoungWriters
Est.1991

YOUNG WRITERS INFORMATION

We hope you have enjoyed reading this book – and that you will continue to in the coming years.

If you're a young writer who enjoys reading and creative writing, or the parent of an enthusiastic poet or story writer, do visit our website **www.youngwriters.co.uk**. Here you will find free competitions, workshops and games, as well as recommended reads, a poetry glossary and our blog.

If you would like to order further copies of this book, or any of our other titles, then please give us a call or visit **www.youngwriters.co.uk**.

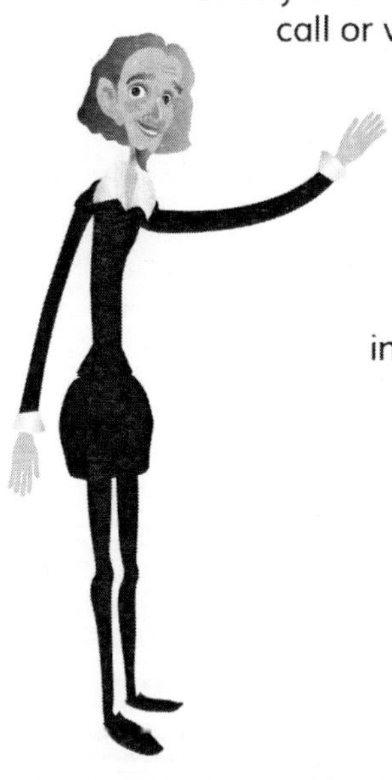

Young Writers
Remus House
Coltsfoot Drive
Peterborough
PE2 9BF
(01733) 890066
info@youngwriters.co.uk